T0038197

Nixology

Nixology

WRITTEN BY
Elouise Anders

ILLUSTRATED BY
Claudia Frittitta

Smith
Street
Books

CONTENTS

Stirred

Booze-free concoctions
stirred to perfection

Shaken

Non-alcoholic favourites
to shake things up

Sipped

Low-alcohol cocktails
to keep spirits high

Shared

Zero-proof pitchers
to share with friends

Syrups

INTRODUCTION

There's a time for a lemonade, and a time for a margarita. Occasions all have their perfect drink, whether that's a brunch spent sipping mimosas into the late afternoon, an evening curled up on the couch with a hot toddy, or a summertime party where condensation drips down the sides of the negronis. Sometimes, a simple soda or juice hits the spot, but there are the times when you want something to mark a moment. You don't need alcohol, however, to make a day special.

What you need is something delicious, prepared with the care that you put into traditional cocktails. In recent history, mocktails were limited to sugar-laden options that suited children's menus more than black-tie events. Today, we're enjoying the popular exploration of boozeless concoctions and the rise of non-alcoholic spirits available for purchase. Whether you're after low or no alcohol, there's never been a better time to order from the bar without feeling like you're missing out.

With the creative use of ingredients, from marmalades to syrups and teas, low-to-no alcohol cocktails playfully reinvent traditional staples and introduce new options that pack a punch, whether or not they're built with alcohol. These drinks reverse traditional ratios, lean on low-ABV liqueurs or sub in new players like tea to create a full-bodied, non-alcoholic drink. The recipes in this book don't taste identical to their high-ABV counterparts, but that doesn't mean they aren't delicious.

Nixology features 60 drinks and plenty of classics, including boozeless plays on the clover cub (page 14), margarita (page 26), whiskey sour (page 41) and mojito (page 65). The recipes in the first three chapters contain no alcohol, if you choose to skip the bitters and use an alcohol-free vanilla extract (see page 9).The fourth chapter features low-alcohol options, including the Michelada (page 111), Bamboo (page 131) and Negroni sbagliato (page 108).

Cocktails can make any occasion feel more special, but you don't need alcohol. The right ingredients, a bit of flair while shaking and a coupe served with a garnish are enough to produce a drink worth raising in a toast. Whatever the occasion, there's a low-proof drink that's perfect.

NOTES ON ABV

All recipes in Sipped are low-ABV, coming in at one standard drink maximum. ABV, or alcohol by volume, is the standard for measuring just how boozy that negroni is. Beers have the lowest ABV, spirits the highest. A non-alcoholic drink should sit under 0.5%.

There is no hard standard defining low-alcohol drinks, but they have signatures. They limit high-proof spirits like gin or vodka, if they include any. Often, drinks with high-proof ingredients are served as highballs, which dilutes the alcohol.

Low-ABV drinks may riff on the original or flip the ratios of high and low-ABV ingredients. The Reverse Manhattan (page 115) is a popular drink that's been flipped (the results are still delicious).

Low-ABV bartending takes advantage of liqueurs and fortified wines to deliver well-rounded drinks. With a bit of Campari, vermouth and creativity, you can mix something delicious.

Spirits

High-proof spirits are used in low quantities in *Nixology*. If you'd like to avoid spirits altogether, several brands distil non-alcoholic liquor.

Bitters

Bitters appear throughout this book. While they do have a high proof, the amount used in these recipes creates a negligible ABV. When bitters are used in the first three chapters, the ABV remains under 0.5%, which is comparable to a bottle of kombucha. Drinks with an ABV this low are regarded as non-alcoholic. For anyone who'd like to completely forgo alcohol, glycerin-based bitters are a great alternative. Some companies do use trace amounts of alcohol in their flavours, but there are others that leave it out.

Vanilla extract

Like bitters, vanilla extract contains alcohol, but the amount used in these recipes means the ABV is under 0.5%. Alcohol-free vanilla extract is available if you'd like to keep your ABV at 0%.

NOTES ON FINISHES

While alcohol may be absent in 0% ABV drinks, there's no reason that presentation needs to go out the window. The right finishes can make even a simple glass of apple juice feel special. A cocktail glass, a salted rim and a flourish of fruit will give any drink the presence of a high-proof classic.

Garnishes

This is the easiest way to glam up your drink. For a wheel, lie your fruit of choice on its side and slice into rounds about 5 mm (¼ in) thick. For a wedge, just cut a citrus in half lengthways, then slice into half circles. And for larger fruit, like melon or pineapple, wedges are a great choice; first cut into thick slices, then cut the slices into wedges and cut an incision. Slide your garnish onto the lip of the glass and admire the finish.

Rims

Not only does a rim add a bit of drama to a drink's presentation, but it also elevates the flavours. The obvious option for rims is salt, but sugar and cinnamon is a delicious combo for spiced drinks, while options like Tajin introduce a kick of spice. While you can experiment and use ingredients like toasted black sesame seeds, most rims use ingredients that you already have lying around to great effect.

Expressing

If you're using citrus peels, always remember to express: this will mist your drink with citrus oils. It's a step that's easy to skip, but it's always worth it for the elevated taste.

With a sharp knife, carefully separate a strip of rind from your citrus fruit of choice, discarding any pith. Trim the edges and twist the strip over the drink so that the oil in the rind sprays into the glass. Rub the twist around the rim of the glass and drop it into the drink.

Shaken

SHAMROCK CLUB

SERVES 1

30 ml (1 fl oz) chilled tonic water

4 teaspoons lemon juice

4 teaspoons Raspberry syrup (page 145)

1 egg white or 30 ml (1 fl oz) aquafaba

ice cubes

3 raspberries on a cocktail stick, to garnish

A play on the gin classic: the clover club. The original arrived on the cocktail scene early, and its raspberry syrup pink has had staying power. That's thanks, in part, to a sweetness that doesn't overpower and a foamy head that's the perfect textural complement. This version swaps gin for tonic, with all the palpability and none of the booze.

.

Place the tonic water, lemon juice, raspberry syrup and egg white or aquafaba in a cocktail shaker, and dry shake for 15 seconds. Add ice and shake for another 15 seconds.

Strain into a chilled coupe and place the prepared cocktail stick across the top of the glass.

COSMONOT

SERVES 1

I couldn't help but wonder if a cosmopolitan needed vodka. In terms of taste, it doesn't. To avoid a drink that simply mixes juice with more juice, this recipe features orange blossom water and marmalade. The latter may sound strange to the uninitiated, but bartenders have used this tangy ingredient since at least the early 1900s; it's as delicious in a cocktail glass as it is spread on toast.

•

1 teaspoon good-quality orange marmalade

90 ml (3 fl oz) cranberry juice

30 ml (1 fl oz) lime juice

2 teaspoons orange blossom water

ice cubes

chilled sparkling water, to top

lime twist, to garnish

In a cocktail shaker, stir the marmalade into the cranberry juice until it dissolves. Add the lime juice, orange blossom water and ice, then shake for 30 seconds until well combined. Strain into a chilled cocktail glass and top with sparkling water.

Serve garnished with a lime twist.

ORGEATTO SOUR

SERVES 1

A traditional amaretto sour relies on its namesake for its distinctive almond taste. To replace amaretto liqueur, this recipe experiments with orgeat: a rich, almond-flavoured syrup that's used in tiki cocktails. A batch of it will serve you well and prove that you don't need alcohol to create drinks with rich bodies.

.

80 ml (⅓ cup) pineapple juice

40 ml (1½ fl oz) lemon juice

4 teaspoons Orgeat syrup (page 148)

2 Luxardo maraschino cherries on a cocktail stick, to garnish

1 egg white or 30 ml (1 fl oz) aquafaba

ice cubes

lemon twist, to garnish

In a cocktail shaker, add the juices, orgeat syrup, 1 teaspoon of syrup from the maraschino cherry jar, and the egg white or aquafaba. Dry shake for 15 seconds, then add ice and shake for another 15 seconds.

Strain into an old-fashioned glass and garnish with the maraschino cherries and a lemon twist.

BITTER SALTY DOG

SERVES 1

Salty dogs may or may not call for Campari, and the liquor choice is up to you: gin or vodka? Mixology is often a choose-your-own adventure and, in this one, we're setting sail with Sanbitter. The Italian soda's bitter notes of grapefruit and orange, which mimic Campari, are a natural choice to recreate the cocktail. The salty rim balances the palate as you sip the afternoon away.

•

Himalayan pink salt, to garnish

2 grapefruit wedges

ice cubes, plus 1 large cube to garnish

45 ml (1½ fl oz) Sanbitter

100 ml (3½ fl oz) pink grapefruit juice

Sprinkle some salt onto a small plate. Run a grapefruit wedge around the rim of an old-fashioned glass and dip the rim into the salt to coat. Place the large ice cube in the glass.

Fill a cocktail shaker with ice. Add the Sanbitter and grapefruit juice, and shake for 30 seconds. Strain into the prepared glass.

Garnish with the remaining grapefruit wedge.

LIME & BASIL SMASH

SERVES 1

zest of 1 lime, plus 2 wedges and 20 ml (¾ fl oz) juice

1 tablespoon caster (superfine) sugar

ice cubes

small bunch of basil (about 10 leaves), plus a sprig to garnish

1 tablespoon Sugar syrup (page 142)

ice cubes

chilled sparkling water, to top

Citrus? Fruit? Herbs? They all have their place in a smash, an icy cocktail that takes many forms. That mutability makes it the perfect candidate for a mocktail, with free rein when it comes to what goes in the shaker. This iteration features lime and basil: a herbaceous, fresh concoction for those lacking sweet tooths.

•

Make a lime–sugar garnish by mixing the lime zest and sugar together on a small plate. Run a lime wedge around the rim of a rocks glass, then press the rim into the lime and sugar mixture to coat. Fill the glass with ice.

Place the basil leaves in a cocktail shaker and muddle gently. Add the sugar syrup and lime juice, then fill the shaker with ice and shake for 30 seconds. Strain into the prepared glass, top with sparkling water and garnish with a sprig of basil and the remaining lime wedge.

HIBISCUS SOUR

SERVES 1

The hibiscus flower's tartness is reminiscent of cranberries and pomegranates, which makes it a popular cocktail ingredient to experiment with. The blooms can be purchased in syrup, which will enhance your drink's flavour and aesthetic. Balanced with agave, this sour is the perfect drink to impress guests (or yourself).

1 hibiscus teabag or
1 tablespoon loose
hibiscus tea

250 ml (1 cup) boiling water

1 tablespoon agave syrup

4 teaspoons lemon juice

1 egg white or 30 ml (1 fl oz)
aquafaba

jar of hibiscus flowers in syrup,
1 flower gently removed from
the jar to garnish

Combine the teabag or loose hibiscus and water in a teapot. Steep for 3–4 minutes, then strain into a heatproof container and discard the hibiscus. Refrigerate until cold.

In a cocktail shaker, add the agave syrup, lemon juice, egg white or aquafaba, 1 tablespoon of hibiscus syrup from the jar and 60 ml (¼ cup) of the hibiscus tea.

Dry shake for 15 seconds, then add ice and shake for another 15 seconds. Strain into a chilled coupe and garnish with the hibiscus flower.

TIMMY'S MARGARITA
SERVES 1

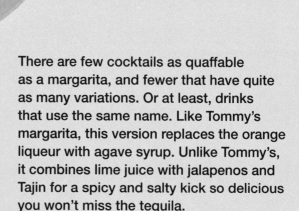

There are few cocktails as quaffable as a margarita, and fewer that have quite as many variations. Or at least, drinks that use the same name. Like Tommy's margarita, this version replaces the orange liqueur with agave syrup. Unlike Tommy's, it combines lime juice with jalapenos and Tajin for a spicy and salty kick so delicious you won't miss the tequila.

•

Tajin seasoning

2 lime wedges

ice cubes

30 ml (1 fl oz) lime juice

30 ml (1 fl oz) orange juice

1 tablespoon Jalapeno syrup (page 146)

2 teaspoons agave syrup

chilled sparkling water, to top

a few thin slices of jalapeno (seeds optional), to garnish

Sprinkle 1 tablespoon of Tajin onto a small plate. Run one lime wedge around the rim of a rocks glass and dip the rim into the Tajin to coat. Fill the glass with ice.

Add a pinch of Tajin with the juices and syrups to a cocktail shaker. Fill with ice and shake for 30 seconds, then strain into the prepared glass.

Top with sparkling water and garnish with the jalapeno slices and the second lime wedge.

POMEGRANATE MULE

SERVES 1

A ruby red riff on the cocktail classic. There's no need to purchase copper mugs to serve a mule, though the metal will keep your drink cooler and enhance the flavour. Served in a glass, this mix of pomegranate and ginger beer is still delicious.

.

Fill a cocktail shaker with ice. Pour in the pomegranate and lime juices, and shake for 15 seconds. Strain into a rocks glass filled with ice.

Top with ginger beer and sprinkle with the pomegranate seeds.

ice cubes

60 ml (¼ cup) pomegranate juice

1 tablespoon lime juice

chilled ginger beer, to top

1 tablespoon pomegranate seeds, to garnish

SAGE & CITRUS

SERVES 1

30 ml (1 fl oz) lime juice

1 tablespoon agave syrup

2 sage leaves

100 ml (3½ fl oz) blood orange juice

ice cubes

chilled sparkling water, to top

blood orange wheel, to garnish

Sage is useful for more than just savoury dishes. Its earthy tones introduce a herbal note to drinks, which pairs particularly well with citrus. Here, we use blood orange – the fruit is tart, sweet and the perfect shade of red to make a drink that looks and tastes delicious.

•

Place the lime juice, agave syrup and sage leaves in a cocktail shaker. Gently muddle the leaves, then add the orange juice and ice. Shake well for 30 seconds, then strain into a rocks glass filled with ice.

Top with sparkling water and garnish with a blood orange wheel.

PASSION-TINI

SERVES 1

Is this a martini? No. Is it delicious? Yes. Love or hate its alcoholic counterpart's name (the pornstar), it's still a popular drink for a reason: the blend of vanilla and passionfruit is delicious. Muddled pineapple adds an extra layer that makes this drink a crowd favourite.

•

pulp of 2 passionfruit, plus ½ passionfruit to garnish

2.5 cm (1 in) thick pineapple slice, cored and roughly chopped

1 tablespoon cloudy apple juice

1 tablespoon lime juice

1 tablespoon Vanilla syrup (page 142)

ice cubes

Strain half of the passionfruit pulp through a fine-mesh sieve into a bowl, using a spoon to push any juice through. Discard the solids.

In a cocktail shaker, muddle the pineapple. Add the passionfruit puree and pulp, apple juice, lime juice, vanilla syrup and ice. Shake vigorously for 30 seconds, then double strain into a chilled cocktail glass.

Garnish with a passionfruit half.

SPRINGTIME FIZZ

SERVES 1

1 chamomile teabag
or 1 tablespoon loose
chamomile tea

250 ml (1 cup) boiling water

2 teaspoons Honey syrup
(page 143)

2 teaspoons Elderflower syrup
(page 142)

1 teaspoon orange
blossom water

1 tablespoon lemon juice

1 egg white or 30 ml
(1 fl oz) aquafaba

chilled sparkling water, to top

washed chamomile flowers,
to garnish

It doesn't have to be spring for you to
enjoy this drink, but it is perfect paired
with an afternoon in the garden. The floral
notes from the chamomile, elderflower
and orange blossom water are a bouquet
in a glass, with a silky finish to round off
this fizz.

.

Combine the teabag or loose chamomile and
water in a teapot. Steep for 4–5 minutes, then
strain into a heatproof container and discard
the chamomile. Refrigerate until cold.

Add the syrups, orange blossom water, lemon
juice, egg white or aquafaba and 60 ml (¼ cup)
of the chamomile tea to a cocktail shaker. Dry
shake for 15 seconds, then add ice and shake
for a further 15 seconds. Strain into a chilled
cocktail glass and top with sparkling water.

Garnish with chamomile flowers.

JUNIPER & TONIC

SERVES 1

This drink's juniper-forward flavour recreates the classic gin and tonic, which has been prepared since time immemorial (or at least the mid-1800s). Swapping a G for a J, while keeping the T, this recipe preserves the original's botanicals. Left-over syrup can be used to make a Gimlet (page 42).

•

ice cubes

25 ml (¾ fl oz) Juniper syrup (page 143)

1 tablespoon lime juice

cucumber ribbon, to garnish

chilled tonic water, to top

In a cocktail shaker filled with ice, combine the juniper syrup and lime juice. Shake for 15 seconds, then strain into a rocks glass filled with ice.

Weave the cucumber ribbon between the ice cubes, then top with tonic water.

TROPICAL HOT HONEY

SERVES 1

A drink for lovers of spicy sweet heat, made with chilli-infused honey. You can infuse some yourself (page 143), or head to the supermarket or deli for a bottle of hot honey. It's a spicy treat that tastes great on a pizza, in a glass or wherever else you're inspired to drizzle it, even if that's straight-up on a spoon. Just make sure to dilute it into a syrup before mixing it into drinks.

•

2 teaspoons salt

2.5 cm (1 in) thick pineapple slice, cored and roughly chopped, plus a wedge to garnish

4 teaspoons hot honey syrup (page 143)

1 tablespoon lime juice

90 ml (3 fl oz) pineapple juice

2 dashes of chilli bitters (optional; see page 9)

ice cubes

chilled ginger beer, to top

To make a salt solution, combine the salt with 40 ml (1¼ fl oz) of water in a container with a dropper, then seal and shake to combine.

In a cocktail shaker, muddle the pineapple.

Add the honey syrup, juices, salt solution, bitters (if using) and ice, and shake for 30 seconds. Strain into a rocks glass filled with ice and top with ginger beer.

Garnish with a pineapple wedge.

WHISKTEA SOUR

SERVES 1

Is it possible to create a whiskey sour without the whiskey? Many say yes. The maltiness of Assam tea is known to evoke the spirit, particularly when mixed with vanilla. For that, we have science to thank. Whiskey and vanilla share an organic compound – vanillin – which makes the latter a great substitute in mocktails. So, shake one up and raise a glass to chemistry.

1 Assam teabag or 1 teaspoon loose Assam tea

250 ml (1 cup) boiling water

4 teaspoons Vanilla syrup (page 142)

30 ml (1 fl oz) lemon juice

1 egg white or 30 ml (1 fl oz) aquafaba

ice cubes

Luxardo maraschino cherry, to garnish

Combine the teabag or loose-leaf tea and water in a teapot. Steep for 30 seconds, then strain into a heatproof container and discard the teabag or leaves. Refrigerate until cold.

In a cocktail shaker, combine the vanilla syrup, lemon juice, egg white or aquafaba and 60 ml (¼ cup) of the tea. Dry shake for 15 seconds, then add ice and shake for another 15 seconds.

Strain into an old-fashioned glass filled with ice and garnish with a maraschino cherry.

GIMLET

SERVES 1

A gimlet combines lime cordial with gin. Neither are in sight here. Instead, juniper syrup recreates the liquor's herbaceous, botanical notes. To avoid weighing the drink down with sugar, lime juice replaces the cordial. Cocktail pedants might shake their heads, but this play on the classic goes down just fine.

•

20 ml (¾ fl oz) Juniper syrup (page 143)

30 ml (1 fl oz) lime juice

ice cubes

chilled sparkling water, to top

lime wheel, to garnish

Pour the juniper syrup and lime juice into a cocktailer shaker filled with ice. Shake for 15 seconds, then strain into a chilled cocktail glass and top with sparkling water.

Serve garnished with a lime wheel.

Stirred

BALSAMIC STRAWBERRY FIZZ

SERVES 1

4 teaspoons lime juice

1 tablespoon Sugar syrup
(page 142)

¼ teaspoon balsamic vinegar

3 basil leaves

4 strawberries, hulled and
quartered

chilled sparkling water, to top

basil sprig, to garnish

If you've never tried balsamic vinegar and
strawberries together, this drink will be a
revelation. If you have, you'll be pleasantly
surprised to learn the classic pairing works
just as well stirred in a glass. The acidic notes
enhance the sweet. Muddled together, they
taste gourmet.

•

Place the lime juice, sugar syrup, balsamic
vinegar, basil leaves and strawberries in a
mixing glass and muddle. Transfer to a glass
filled with ice, top with sparkling water and
stir well.

Serve garnished with a basil sprig.

NOGRONI

SERVES 1

If you're after a simpler solution to the negroni, you can use equal parts non-alcoholic gin, bitter concentrate syrup and non-alcoholic sweet vermouth, with a few dashes of zero-proof bitters. If you're feeling more adventurous, try this recipe, which riffs on the original. Whatever you choose, remember to express the peel.

•

2 teaspoons Juniper syrup (see page 143)

30 ml (1 fl oz) Sanbitter

30 ml (1 fl oz) pomegranate juice

1 dash of blood orange bitters (optional; see page 9)

ice cubes

orange twist, to garnish

Add the juniper syrup, Sanbitter, pomegranate juice and bitters (if using) to a mixing glass filled with ice, and stir until chilled.

Strain into a rocks glass filled with ice and garnish with an orange twist.

NEW FASHIONED

SERVES 1

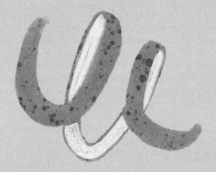

1 barley teabag

1 sugar cube

1 dash of Angostura bitters
(see page 9) or 3 dashes of
non-alcoholic bitters

ice cubes

orange twist, to garnish

Luxardo maraschino cherry on
a cocktail stick, to garnish

To remake the old fashioned, a new trick: barley tea. Like the Whisktea sour (page 41), tea is used here to mimic the complexity of the liquor. Does it taste the same as bourbon? No. Does it make for a great drink? Yes. If you've already prepared Assam tea for a whisktea sour, you can swap it in for the barley tea.

•

Fill a container with 1 litre (4 cups) of water. Add the teabag, cover and refrigerate for 2 hours. Discard the teabag.

Place the sugar cube on the bottom of an old-fashioned glass, add the bitters and muddle. Add 80 ml (⅓ cup) of the barley tea and a few ice cubes. Stir until chilled and garnish with an orange twist and the maraschino cherry.

The remaining barley tea can be kept in an airtight container in the fridge for up to 4 days.

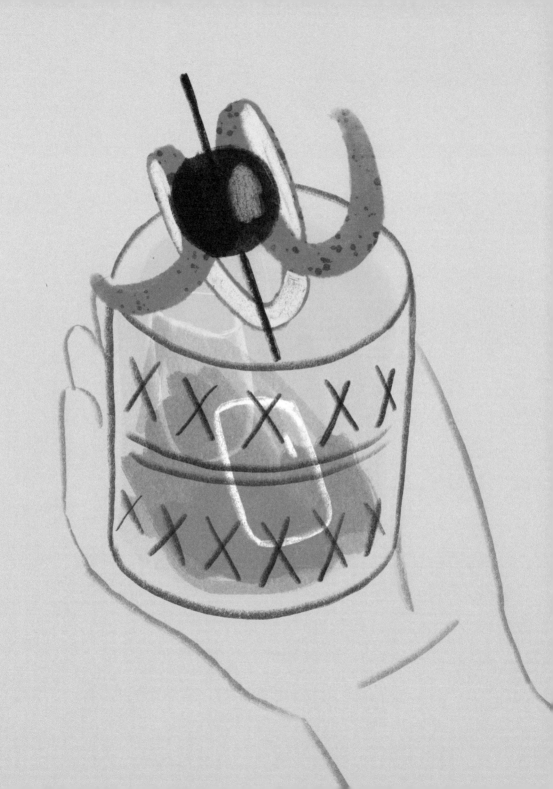

PALOMA
SERVES 1

The Mexican classic, without the tequila. If you'd like to recreate the cocktail more closely, adding 45 ml (1½ fl oz) of a non-alcoholic tequila will do the trick. With or without the spirit, however, this a refreshing, bright drink that will leave you smacking your lips.

•

sea salt

2 pink grapefruit wedges, plus 90 ml (3 fl oz) juice

ice cubes

1 tablespoon agave syrup

1 tablespoon lime juice

chilled sparkling water, to top

Sprinkle some salt onto a small plate. Run a grapefruit wedge around the rim of a tall glass and dip the rim into the salt to coat. Fill the glass with ice.

Pour the agave syrup, lime juice and grapefruit juice into the glass, top with sparkling water and stir well.

Garnish with the remaining grapefruit wedge.

GUNNER

SERVES 1

The gunner doesn't require experimentation – this drink was non-alcoholic from the get-go. With origins in Hong Kong, this ginger-laden glass is extremely sippable and will get you through the hottest days of summer.

ice cubes

1 dash of Angostura bitters (see page 9) or 3 dashes of non-alcoholic bitters

1 teaspoon Lime syrup (page 149)

2–3 lime wheels, to garnish

125 ml (½ cup) ginger ale

125 ml (½ cup) ginger beer

•

Fill a tall glass with ice.

Add the bitters and lime syrup, and stir to combine. Add the lime wheels, followed by the ginger ale and beer, and stir again to finish.

MINT SPRIG

SERVES 1

Grenadine, it may surprise some, is not produced from cherries – it's made with pomegranates. A longstanding classic in drinks with or without alcohol, it makes a delicious partner here for cucumber and mint. Refreshing and just the right amount of sweet, the mint sprig is a boozeless pick-me-up.

•

1 short cucumber, peeled and roughly chopped

30 ml (1 fl oz) lime juice

4 teaspoons grenadine

2 teaspoons Sugar syrup (page 142)

crushed ice

chilled sparkling water, to top

mint sprig and cucumber ribbons, to garnish

Put the cucumber in a blender and blitz to a fine mixture. Strain through a sieve lined with muslin (cheesecloth) into a small bowl, discarding the solids.

Combine the lime juice, grenadine, sugar syrup and 60 ml (¼ cup) of the cucumber juice in a tall glass filled with crushed ice. Top with sparkling water and stir to combine.

Garnish with a mint sprig and cucumber ribbons.

SOBER MARY

SERVES 1

250 ml (1 cup) chilled tomato juice

1 large parsley sprig

1 large coriander (cilantro) sprig

1 teaspoon salt

½ teaspoon celery salt, plus extra to season

⅛ teaspoon cayenne pepper

1 lemon wedge, plus 3 teaspoons juice

ice cubes

45 ml (1½ fl oz) pickle juice

Worcestershire sauce, to taste

Tabasco, to taste

celery stalk, to garnish

green olive, cocktail onion and cornichon on a cocktail stick, to garnish

Most Bloody Marys are so flavour-packed that you'd be hard-pressed to notice vodka's presence – or absence. This recipe's blitzed herbs, celery salt, pickle juice, cayenne pepper, Tabasco and garnishes are more than enough to wake you up at brunch, whether you're chasing the hair of the dog or just a kick of heat.

•

Place the tomato juice, parsley and coriander in a blender, and blitz until the herbs are very fine and the mixture is well combined.

In a small bowl, mix the salts and cayenne pepper. Run the lemon wedge around the rim of a tall glass, then dip the rim into the salt mixture to coat.

Fill the glass with ice and add the pickle juice, lemon juice and herb mixture. Add celery salt, freshly ground black pepper, Worcestershire sauce and Tabasco to taste, stirring as you go.

Garnish with a celery stalk and the prepared cocktail stick.

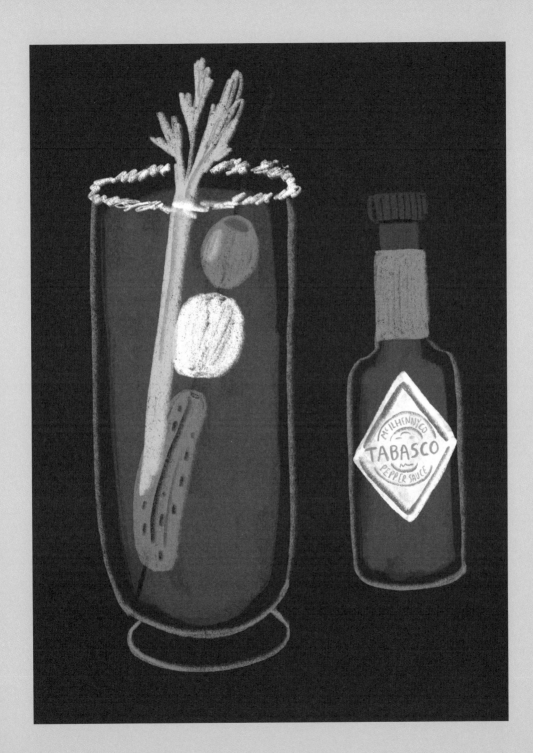

CAIPIRINHA

SERVES 1

Brazil's national drink traditionally features cachaça, which is made from sugar cane juices. To recreate its distinct flavour, non-alcoholic spirits are a common solution. This delicious alternative keeps things simple and swaps in ginger beer for a refreshing, inexpensive glass.

•

1 lime, cut into 12 pieces, plus a wheel to garnish

1 tablespoon soft brown sugar

ice cubes

chilled ginger beer, to top

ice cubes

Muddle the lime and sugar in a mixing glass. Transfer into an old-fashioned glass filled with ice and top with ginger beer.

Stir to combine, and serve garnished with a lime wheel.

LEMON-LIME SUNRISE

SERVES 1

It might not be the same drink the Rolling Stones ordered in the 1970s, but orange juice and grenadine still create a beautiful gradient in a glass without the tequila. For those after a less-sweet hit, swap out the lemon-lime soda with non-alcoholic sparkling white wine or sparkling water.

1 tablespoon lime juice

90 ml (3 fl oz) orange juice

ice cubes

1 tablespoon grenadine

chilled lemon-lime soda, to top

maraschino cherry, to garnish

orange slice, to garnish

Combine the juices in a tall glass filled with ice.

Slowly add the grenadine, pouring against the inside of the glass so that it sinks to the bottom, then top with the lemon-lime soda.

Serve garnished with a cherry and an orange slice.

BLUEBERRY NOJITO

SERVES 1

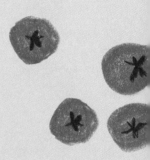

½ lime, cut into 6 pieces, plus a wedge to garnish

1 small handful of mint leaves

155 g (1 cup) fresh blueberries, plus extra to garnish

1 tablespoon Elderflower syrup (page 144)

crushed ice

chilled sparkling water, to top

mint sprig, to garnish

Does the mojito trace back to the 16th century? Maybe. Did it include blueberries back then? Probably not. This fruity adaptation goes a step further and adds Elderflower syrup (page 144) into the mix. It may not be historically accurate, but it's a flavour combination worth adding to the history books.

•

Muddle the lime, mint, blueberries and elderflower syrup in a mixing glass. Transfer to a tall glass and add crushed ice. Top with sparkling water, and stir to combine.

Garnish with a mint sprig.

LIGHT & MILD

SERVES 1

The swirling combination of rum and ginger beer gave the dark 'n' stormy its name. This version experiments with tea and Velvet falernum (page 147) for a full-bodied drink. The latter is a popular tiki cocktail ingredient that introduces a spice and zest that makes for ginger beer's perfect companion.

.

1 English Breakfast teabag or 1 teaspoon loose English Breakfast tea

250 ml (1 cup) boiling water

1 tablespoon lime juice

60 ml (¼ cup) ginger beer

2 drops Salt solution (page 38)

20 ml (¾ fl oz) Velvet falernum syrup (page 147)

crushed ice

lime wedge, to garnish

Combine the teabag or loose tea and water in a teapot. Steep for 3 minutes, then strain into a heatproof container and discard the teabag or leaves. Refrigerate until cold.

Combine the lime juice, ginger beer, salt solution, falernum syrup and 60 ml (¼ cup) of the tea in a tall glass filled with crushed ice and stir to combine.

Garnish with a lime wedge.

GINGER & CUCUMBER MULE

SERVES 1

Ginger three ways: muddled, brewed and candied. For ginger lovers, its kick won't be lacking. Cucumber juice and mint help build the rest of the glass for an aromatic combination that'll taste even better served in a copper mug.

•

1 short cucumber, peeled and roughly chopped

2.5 cm (1 in) piece of ginger, thinly sliced

4 teaspoons lime juice

2 teaspoons Sugar syrup (page 142)

6 mint leaves

ice cubes

chilled ginger beer, to top

candied ginger on a cocktail stick, to garnish

Put the cucumber in a blender and blitz to a fine mixture. Strain through a sieve lined with muslin (cheesecloth) into a small bowl, discarding the solids.

Muddle the ginger in a mixing glass. Add the lime juice, sugar syrup, mint leaves and 60 ml (¼ cup) of the cucumber juice, and gently muddle again. Transfer to a tumbler and add ice. Top with ginger beer and stir well to combine.

Garnish with the prepared cocktail stick.

COCONUT'S MATCH

SERVES 1

With matcha's vibrant green, a rim of black sesame seeds and a coconut garnish on top, this drink delivers on looks. Matcha's vegetal, nutty notes are paired with maple syrup and coconut milk for an indulgent, creamy drink that's healthier than it tastes.

•

In a small frying pan over medium–low heat, toast the sesame seeds for 3–4 minutes, until fragrant. Transfer the seeds to a small plate to cool completely.

On another small plate, pour 1 tablespoon of maple syrup. Dip the rim of a tall glass into the syrup, then press into the toasted sesame seeds to coat.

In a heatproof glass, combine the hot water and matcha, stirring until the matcha is completely dissolved. Allow to cool slightly, then pour into the prepared glass. Add the rest of the maple syrup, coconut milk and ice, and stir until chilled.

Garnish with shredded coconut.

1 tablespoon black
sesame seeds

1½ tablespoons maple syrup

1½ teaspoons matcha powder

100 ml (3½ fl oz) hot water

250 ml (1 cup) coconut milk

ice cubes

shredded coconut, to garnish

LAVENDER & CUCUMBER SMASH

SERVES 1

A drink that's made to impress, featuring lavender's signature scent. The flower can overpower if you use too much, so you're best to taste as you go. In the right proportions, it's a lovely floral complement to this smash's fresh cucumber.

•

1 short cucumber, peeled and roughly chopped

60 ml (¼ cup) chilled tonic water

4 teaspoons Lavender Syrup (page 144)

crushed ice

edible lavender sprigs, to garnish

Put the cucumber in a blender and blitz to a fine mixture. Strain through a sieve lined with muslin (cheesecloth) into a small bowl, discarding the solids.

Pour the tonic water, lavender syrup and 60 ml (¼ cup) of the cucumber water into a rocks glass, and stir well.

Top with crushed ice and garnish with lavender sprigs.

Shared

SANSGRIA

SERVES 8

1 apple, peeled, cored and sliced into small chunks

1 orange, sliced, plus 8 orange wheels to garnish

1 lemon, sliced

1 tablespoon caster (superfine) sugar

1 bottle non-alcoholic red wine

125 ml (½ cup) orange juice

125 ml (½ cup) cranberry juice

ice cubes

chilled sparkling water, to top

A drink made for parties, or when you have a less-than-desirable bottle of wine. Infused with fruit and sweetened with sugar, sangria turns an okay red into a great bowl of punch, alcoholic or not. Inspired to experiment? This is a great drink to practise a bit of creativity on. Add seasonal fruits and a pick a non-alcoholic wine with complementary notes.

•

Place the fruit and sugar in a large pitcher. Stir well to combine, then pour in the wine and juices. Set aside in the fridge for at least 4 hours or, preferably, overnight.

Add a few ice cubes to the sansgria just before serving and top with sparkling water. Give everything a final stir, then pour into punch glasses and garnish each with an orange wheel.

BLACKBERRY FIZZ

SERVES 8

If you're looking for a drink to share at the picnic, this blackberry fizz is the perfect choice, full of syrup made from fresh berries. It's easy to customise; use ginger ale for extra sweetness, and add tarragon or lavender for a herbal kick. Whatever you choose, it'll be delicious.

•

120 ml (4 fl oz) Blackberry syrup (page 146)

crushed ice

chilled sparkling water or ginger ale, to top

lemon or lime slices, to serve

tarragon leaves or edible lavender sprigs, to garnish (optional)

Pour a tablespoon of the blackberry syrup into each glass.

Add crushed ice, then top with the sparkling water and stir to combine. Garnish with citrus slices and tarragon or lavender, if desired.

PEACH BELLINI

SERVES 8

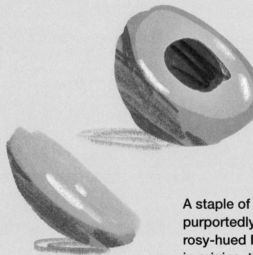

A staple of brunches, with a namesake purportedly inspired by Giovanni Bellini's rosy-hued Renaissance paintings. Venetian in origins, this blend of sparkling wine and peach puree is always a welcome weekend treat, though this bellini's lack of alcohol means it can be enjoyed any morning.

•

2 peaches, pitted and roughly diced

1 tablespoon lemon juice

1 teaspoon caster (superfine) sugar

1 chilled bottle non-alcoholic sparkling white wine

Blitz the peach, lemon juice and sugar in a food processor until smooth. Strain the puree through a fine-meshed sieve into a bowl, discarding the solids.

Divide the puree among eight champagne flutes and top with the sparkling wine.

BUBBLY PEAR PUNCH

SERVES 8

250 ml (1 cup) pear nectar

2 tablespoons freshly grated ginger

25 ml (¾ fl oz) lemon juice

1 bottle chilled non-alcoholic sparkling white wine

fresh cranberries, to garnish

8 rosemary sprigs, to garnish

When the days get colder, ginger and pear are a warming combo. The kick from the ginger lifts this sparkling punch and is delicious matched with the pear's sweeter notes. Garnish yours with cranberries and rosemary sprigs for a perfectly festive set of glasses.

.

Combine the pear nectar, ginger and lemon juice and stir to combine.

Divide the mixture among eight champagne tulips and top with the wine. Skewer a couple of cranberries onto each rosemary sprig and divide among the glasses.

STRAWBERRY DAIQUIRI

SERVES 6–8

500 g (1 lb 2 oz) fresh strawberries, hulled and cut in half, plus slices to garnish

145 g (⅔ cup) caster (superfine) sugar

80 ml (⅓ cup) lemon juice

600 g (1 lb 5 oz) frozen strawberries

80 ml (⅓ cup) lime juice

80 ml (⅓ cup) Sugar syrup (page 142)

10 basil leaves

540 g (4 cups) ice cubes

6–8 lime wheels, to garnish

There are few better uses for a blender than a daiquiri. This version is at its best when strawberries are in season, so don't let the chance pass you by. Stock up on fresh berries and get your blender ready to whip up some delicious frozen drinks.

In a small bowl, combine the fresh strawberries with the sugar and lemon juice. Cover and refrigerate for 30 minutes.

Place the sugared strawberries in a high-speed blender, followed by the frozen strawberries, lime juice, sugar syrup and basil leaves. Add the ice and blend at high speed until smooth.

Pour into six to eight large cocktail glasses and garnish each with a lime wheel and sliced strawberries.

PINEAPPLE AGUA FRESCA

SERVES 8

Agua frescas are common in Mexico, where these non-alcoholic drinks are easy to find, often sold by street vendors. Lighter than a juice, these refreshing blends of fruit, water and sugar are the perfect solution when you need a drink you can prepare ahead of time. For lovers of pineapple, this is a delicious option.

.

1 kg (2 lb 3 oz) pineapple flesh, roughly chopped

60–80 ml (¼–⅓ cup) lime juice, to taste

80 ml (⅓ cup) Sugar syrup (page 142)

1 lime, sliced into thin wedges

6 lemon verbena sprigs, plus extra to garnish

ice cubes

Put the pineapple in a blender and blitz into a fine puree. Strain through a fine-meshed sieve into a bowl, discarding the solids.

Pour the pineapple juice, lime juice and sugar syrup into a large container. Add the lime wedges, verbena sprigs and 1.8 litres (61 fl oz) of water. Stir well and taste, adding more lime juice or sugar syrup, if desired. Refrigerate until chilled.

To serve, pour into ice-filled glasses and garnish with extra verbena sprigs.

MANGO DAIQUIRI

SERVES 4

4 mangos, halved, stones discarded

240 ml (8 fl oz) coconut water

80 ml (⅓ cup) mango juice

120 ml (4 fl oz) lime juice

80 ml (⅓ fl oz) Sugar syrup (page 142)

270 g (2 cups) crushed ice

4 lime wheels, to garnish

Frozen daiquiris don't require alcohol to be delicious. The same can be said of mangoes. This recipe might be unfaithful to a classic daiquiri, which never sees a blender (or fruit, for that matter), but a mango daiquiri is the best drink to pair with a pool or beach. Blended with coconut water, this recipe is perfectly tropical.

•

Scoop the flesh from the mango cheeks and place in a high-speed blender with the coconut water, juices, sugar syrup and ice. Blend at high speed until smooth.

Pour into four large cocktail glasses and garnish each with a lime wheel.

SPARKLING MELON SANSGRIA

SERVES 6–8

Though less immediately identifiable as a traditional sangria, sangria blanco is just as delicious. Made with white wine (and, in this recipe, a sparkling non-alcoholic option), it's a chance to use fruit that wouldn't work as well with red wine. Here, we use melons.

•

Start this recipe the day before serving.

Use a melon baller to ball all three melons – you should have about 2 cups of each fruit. Place the balls in a pitcher and add the Moscato, then gently stir. Cover and refrigerate overnight.

When ready to serve, add the sparkling wine, ginger ale and mint, and stir gently to combine. To serve, use a ladle to give everyone some fruit in their drink.

1 small honeydew melon, seeded

1 small rockmelon (cantaloupe), seeded

½ small seedless watermelon

1 bottle non-alcoholic Moscato wine

1 bottle chilled non-alcoholic sparkling white wine

250 ml (1 cup) chilled dry ginger ale

small bunch of mint, leaves picked

FROZEN BLUEBERRY & ROSEMARY MARGARITAS

SERVES 6

450 g (3 cups) frozen blueberries

45 ml (1½ fl oz) Rosemary syrup (page 149)

185 ml (¾ cup) orange juice

60 ml (¼ cup) lime juice

4 teaspoons agave syrup

250 ml (1 cup) sparkling water

270 g (2 cups) ice cubes

6 small rosemary sprigs, to garnish

The margarita is a hard drink to improve upon, but a blender does a pretty good job. For this recipe, frozen blueberries are recommended. They'll whip up a perfect slushie when whirred together with rosemary, lime juice and agave syrup, for an elevated answer to 7/11's flavour options.

.

Place the all the ingredients in blender, except the rosemary sprigs, and blitz to a fine texture.

Divide between six margarita glasses and garnish each with a rosemary sprig.

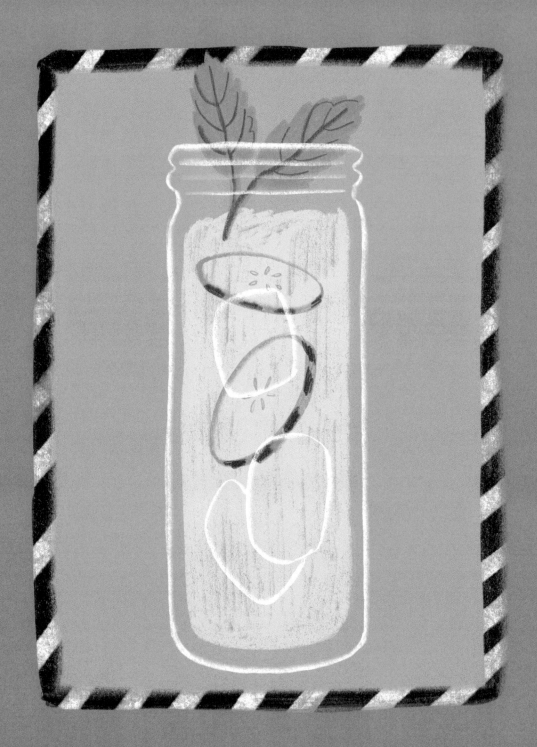

LIME & CUCUMBER AGUA FRESCA

SERVES 4–6

Agua fresca translates to fresh water, and there are few flavours that capture that name better than lime and cucumber. Have a glass, or two, or three: with a whole cucumber mixed in, you'll feel like you've taken a spa trip in a glass. And at the very least, you'll have a very quaffable pitcher.

.

1 long cucumber, roughly chopped

90 ml (3 fl oz) lime juice

90 ml (3 fl oz) Sugar syrup (page 142)

3 mint sprigs

ice cubes

extra mint, lime or cucumber slices, to garnish

Put the cucumber in a blender and blitz to a fine puree. Strain through a sieve lined with muslin (cheesecloth) into a bowl, discarding the solids.

Pour the cucumber juice, lime juice and sugar syrup into a large container. Add the mint sprigs and 1 litre (4 cups) of water. Stir well and taste, adding more lime juice or sugar syrup if desired. Refrigerate until chilled.

To serve, pour into ice-filled glasses and garnish with extra mint, lime or cucumber slices.

BERRY GOOD PUNCH

SERVES 10–12

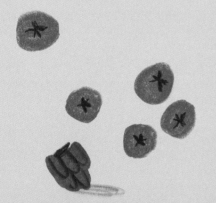

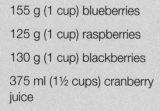

A trick for your next party: swap your ice with frozen fruit. This punch is loaded with berries, which makes for a pretty pitcher when mixed with non-alcoholic sparkling wine. A touch of cranberry and peach juices, and you have the perfect refresher for anyone chasing their five-a-day.

•

155 g (1 cup) blueberries

125 g (1 cup) raspberries

130 g (1 cup) blackberries

375 ml (1½ cups) cranberry juice

185 ml (¾ cup) peach juice

360 g (2 cups) frozen black or purple grapes

1.75 litres (7 cups) non-alcoholic sparkling white wine

Place one-third of the berries in a blender along with 60 ml (¼ cup) of water and blitz to a puree. Strain through a fine-mesh sieve into a bowl, discarding the seeds.

Place the puree in a large pitcher or punch-bowl and add the juices, frozen grapes and remaining berries. Stir well to combine, then top with the sparkling wine

Stir well before serving, using a ladle to give everyone some fruit in their drink.

WATERMELON & BASIL AGUA FRESCA

SERVES 8

When watermelons are close to bursting, basil makes a perfect companion. This drink is as its best when the watermelon is perfectly juicy, to achieve the right sweetness. Add basil to elevate this summertime treat, and sip the heat away as you munch on a slice of melon.

1.5 kg (3 lb 5 oz) seedless watermelon flesh, roughly chopped

80 ml (⅓ cup) lime juice

80 ml (⅓ cup) Sugar syrup (page 142)

1 lime, sliced into wedges

6 purple basil sprigs, plus extra to garnish

ice cubes

Put the watermelon in a blender and blitz to a fine puree. Strain through a sieve lined with muslin (cheesecloth) into a large bowl, discarding the solids.

Pour the watermelon juice, lime juice and sugar syrup into a large container. Add the lime wedges, basil sprigs and 1 litre (4 cups) of water. Stir well and taste, adding more lime juice or sugar syrup, if desired. Refrigerate until chilled.

To serve, pour into ice-filled glasses and garnish with extra basil.

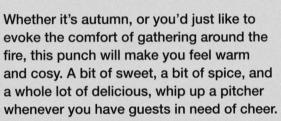

SPICED APPLE PUNCH

SERVES 8–10

handful of crystallised ginger

maple syrup, to finish

½ teaspoon ground cinnamon

1 tablespoon granulated sugar

1.25 litres (5 cups) cloudy apple juice or apple cider

125 ml (½ cup) water

3 cinnamon sticks

6 cloves

¼ teaspoon allspice

1 tablespoon brown sugar

3 cm (1¼ in) piece of ginger, peeled and thinly sliced

½ teaspoon vanilla extract (optional; see page 9)

1 apple, cut into thin slices

Whether it's autumn, or you'd just like to evoke the comfort of gathering around the fire, this punch will make you feel warm and cosy. A bit of sweet, a bit of spice, and a whole lot of delicious, whip up a pitcher whenever you have guests in need of cheer.

Thread some cocktail sticks with one or two chunks of crystallised ginger – enough for your guests – and set aside.

Pour a small amount of maple syrup onto a small plate, then mix the cinnamon and sugar on a second plate. Dip the rim of a glass into the syrup, and then press into the sugar and cinnamon to coat, repeating with each glass.

Pour the apple juice or cider and water into a saucepan and add the spices, brown sugar, fresh ginger and vanilla extract. Bring to the boil, then reduce the heat and simmer for 4–5 minutes, stirring occasionally, until it has reached your desired level of spice. Remove from the heat and add the apple slices.

Serve in heatproof glasses, garnished with the prepared cocktail sticks.

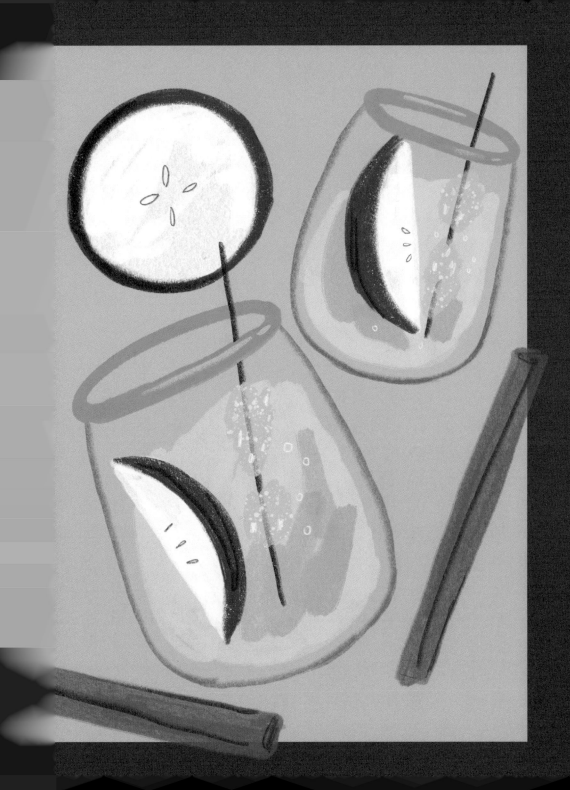

PIÑA COLADA

SERVES 4–6

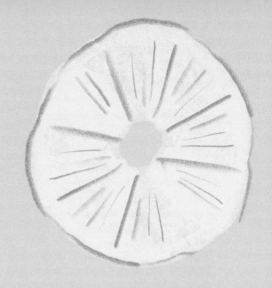

Like other cocktails that put non-alcoholic ingredients forward, the piña colada doesn't suffer from a lack of liquor. At its alcoholic best, this drink features white rum; with a more neutral flavour, the spirit doesn't overpower the other ingredients. In this version, there's nothing getting in the way of that delicious, creamy blend of coconut and pineapple.

•

Put three-quarters of the pineapple (about 750 g/1 lb 11 oz) in a blender, and blitz into a fine puree. Strain through a fine-mesh sieve into a bowl, discarding the solids. Slice the remaining pineapple into wedges and set aside.

Place the coconut cream, syrup and 400 ml (13½ fl oz) of the pineapple juice in a high-speed blender with the ice. Blend until smooth.

Pour into poco grande glasses and garnish with pineapple wedges and leaves.

The remaining pineapple juice will keep in an airtight container in the fridge for 3 days.

1 pineapple (about
1 kg/2 lb 3 oz), peeled
and cored, leaves saved

1 kg (2 lb 3 oz) pineapple flesh

80 ml (⅓ cup) coconut cream

60 ml (¼ fl oz) sugar syrup

540 g (6 cups) crushed ice

PISTACHIO HORCHATA

SERVES 4

250 g (1¼ cups) uncooked jasmine rice

75 g (½ cup) pistachio nuts, plus extra chopped nuts to garnish

1 cinnamon stick, broken into pieces

6 cardamom pods, cracked

1 plump vanilla bean, split in half lengthways, or 2 teaspoons vanilla paste

750 ml (3 cups) boiling water

175 g (½ cup) honey

ice cubes

ground cinnamon, to garnish

Horchata belongs to many countries and takes different forms, depending what soil you're drinking it on. This recipe follows in the Mexican tradition, using rice, cinnamon and sugar to produce a delicious, sweet drink with just the right amount of spice. Pistachios round it off for a glass sure to please any guest.

•

Place the rice, pistachios, cinnamon and cardamom in a large bowl. If using a vanilla bean, add it now. Pour in the boiling water, then cover and set aside to soak for 6–8 hours.

Place the soaked ingredients in a blender and process on high until smooth. Strain into a pitcher through a sieve lined with muslin (cheesecloth), discarding the solids.

Add the honey, 250 ml (1 cup) of cold water and, if using, the vanilla paste. Blend the liquid again, then strain a final time. Taste and adjust the sweetness if desired.

Pour into glasses filled with ice and garnish with chopped pistachio nuts and a sprinkling of ground cinnamon.

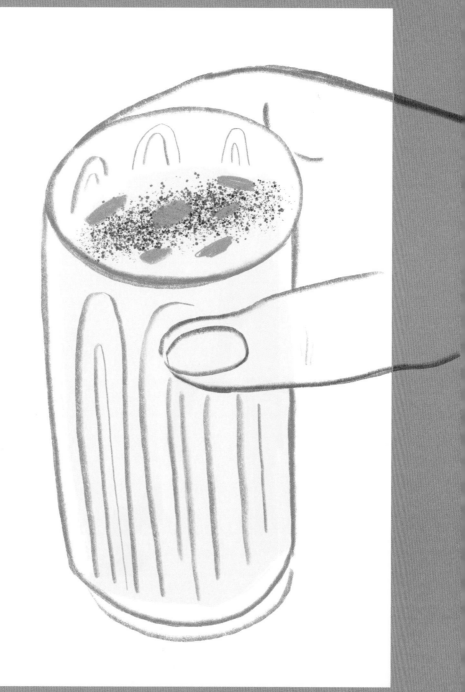

Sipped

NEGRONI SBAGLIATO

SERVES 1

60 ml (¼ cup) chilled non-alcoholic Prosecco or other sparkling white wine

ice cubes

30 ml (1 fl oz) sweet vermouth

1 tablespoon Campari

chilled sparkling water, to top

orange twist, to garnish

This cocktail could just as easily be called an Americano sbagliato. Both are built with Campari and vermouth and finished with a bit of carbonation. In the sbagliato's case, it comes from Prosecco. Born from a happy accident that swapped bubbles in for gin, the negroni sbagliato's effervescent bitterness is worthy of internet virality.

•

Pour the Prosecco into an ice-filled rocks glass. Top with the vermouth and Campari and stir to combine.

Finish with a dash of sparkling water and garnish with an orange twist.

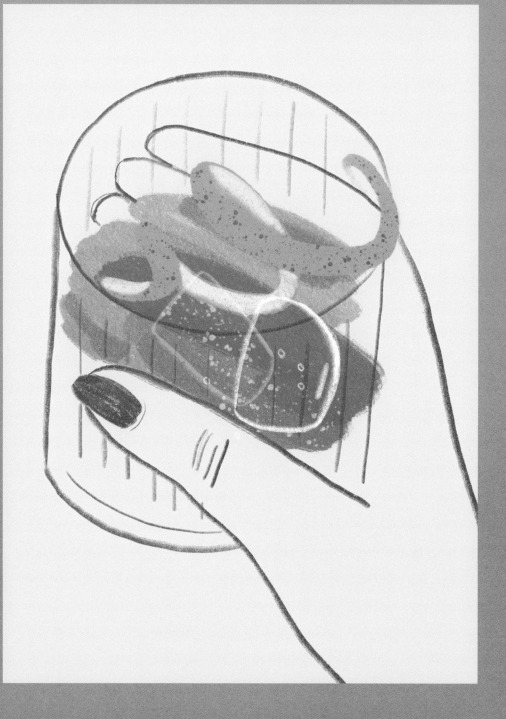

MICHELADA

SERVES 1

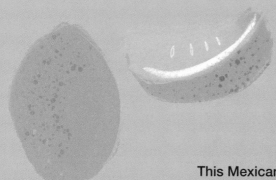

2 teaspoons smoked sea salt flakes

2 lime wedges, plus 1 tablespoon juice

ice cubes

2–3 dashes of hot sauce of your choice

2 dashes of Worcestershire sauce

355 ml (12 fl oz) chilled bottle of light Mexican lager

This Mexican classic doesn't require exact ratios or ingredients. Tomato juice can be added, and the choice of beer is up to you, as is the hot sauce. The result, however, should be a Mexican lager with a kick of heat and citrus that transforms a simple beer into a favourite cocktail.

.

Place the salt on a small plate. Run a lime wedge around the rim of a beer glass, then dip the rim into the salt to coat.

Add ice to the glass, along with the lime juice, hot sauce and Worcestershire sauce. Stir, then pour in the beer and stir again. Garnish with the remaining lime wedge and serve.

APEROL SPRITZ

SERVES 1

The aperitif that swept the world, for good reason. This bittersweet spritz is the perfect drink to sip while you imagine sitting in a Venetian piazza. Finish it with a slice of orange, pair it with some snacks and while away the evening with this fizzy drink.

•

ice cubes

30 ml (1 fl oz) Aperol

60 ml (¼ cup) chilled dry Prosecco

chilled sparkling water, to top

orange wheel, to garnish

1 Sicilian olive on a cocktail stick, to garnish

Fill a large balloon glass with ice. Pour over the Aperol and Prosecco and top with a dash of sparkling water.

Serve garnished with an orange wheel and the olive.

REVERSE MANHATTAN

SERVES 1

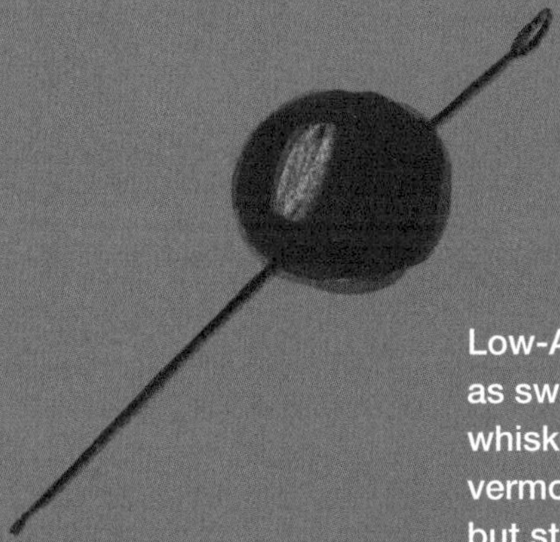

ice cubes

45 ml (1½ fl oz) sweet vermouth

2 teaspoons rye whiskey

1 dash of Angostura bitters

chilled sparkling water, to top

Luxardo maraschino cherry on a cocktail stick, to garnish

Low-ABV solutions are sometimes as simple as swapping ratios. A classic Manhattan places whiskey at the front; the reverse leads with vermouth, for a cocktail that's less heady but still packed with flavour. For those after something sweeter, swap the rye whiskey with bourbon.

In a mixing glass filled with ice, add the vermouth, whiskey and bitters. Stir for 30 seconds until chilled, then strain into a chilled cocktail glass. Top with a dash of sparkling water.

Garnish with the prepared cocktail stick.

ROSE SPRITZER

SERVES 1

ice cubes

90 ml (3 fl oz) chilled
sparkling rose

2 teaspoons Rose petal syrup
(page 142)

60 ml (¼ cup) chilled
sparkling water

fresh rose petals, washed,
or edible dried rose petals,
to garnish

Mixed with sparkling water, this spritzer
gives wine a bubbly lift with rose syrup
added in. With petals floating on top,
it's the perfect drink to impress guests,
to serve at a special occasion or to sip
by yourself in a bathtub.

•

In a wine glass filled with ice, add the rose,
rose petal syrup and sparkling water. Stir well
to combine, then garnish with the rose petals.

SHERRY COBBLER

SERVES 1

60 ml (¼ cup) amontillado sherry

1 tablespoon pineapple juice

1 tablespoon Sugar syrup (see page 142)

2 orange slices

ice cubes, plus crushed ice to garnish

pineapple wedges, seasonal berries and/or mint, to garnish

One of the oldest cocktail classics: sherry cobblers appeared in the 1830s as an American solution to sweltering afternoons. Combing fruit and fortified wine, it's an impressive-looking glass that doesn't require any high-proof spirits or bartending expertise.

•

Add the sherry, pineapple juice, sugar syrup and orange slices to a cocktail shaker filled with ice. Shake vigorously for 30 seconds, then strain into a tall glass filled with crushed ice.

Garnish with your chosen assortment of fruit and/or mint.

SPAGHETT
SERVES 1

This drink is so simple, you don't even need to do dishes. Take a swig from a bottle of beer, add a glug of Aperol, a squeeze of lemon, and you have the spaghett. Your bottle will have a rosy hue and a fruity, tart note that never fails to refresh. For those with a taste for the bitter, swap the Aperol for Campari.

•

30 ml (1 fl oz) Aperol

20 ml (¾ fl oz) lemon juice

355 ml (12 fl oz) chilled bottle of non-alcoholic beer

lemon wedge, to garnish

In a beer glass, add the Aperol and lemon juice. Finish with the beer and stir to combine.

Garnish with a lemon wedge.

PIMM'S CUP

SERVES 1

4 cucumber slices

45 ml (1½ oz) Pimm's No. 1 Cup

1 tablespoon lemon juice

1 orange slice

1 lemon slice

6 mint leaves

2 strawberries, hulled and quartered

ice cubes

90 ml (3 fl oz) lemonade

90 ml (3 fl oz) ginger beer

Synonymous with spending the day next to sporting courts in the UK, Pimm's is a drink meant to be sipped on sunny stretch of grass. Like the Sherry cobbler (page 119), the glass is filled with fruit. A Pimm's cup adds in cucumber, and in this recipe, mixes lemonade and ginger beer.

.

Muddle half of the cucumber slices in a mixing glass. Add in the Pimm's and lemon juice, and stir well to combine. Transfer to a tall glass and add the orange and lemon slices, half the mint and strawberries, and the ice.

Top with the lemonade and ginger beer, stir a final time, then add the remaining mint and strawberries.

SUZE & TONIC

SERVES 1

Suze can be divisive at first sip. The French aperitif, made from the gentian root, has a distinctive yellow hue and an earthy, complex flavour that takes a moment, or a glass, to acquire a taste for. For those who sit with Suze's depth, its citrusy, floral and bitter notes make it a favourite that pairs beautifully with tonic.

ice cubes

45 ml (1½ fl oz) Suze

20 ml (¾ fl oz) lemon juice

2 dashes of Angostura bitters

chilled tonic water, to top

lemon wedge, to garnish

In tall glass filled with ice, add the Suze, lemon juice and bitters. Stir to combine, and top with tonic water.

Serve garnished with a lemon wedge.

AMERICANO

SERVES 1

The martini isn't James Bond's only drink of choice. The Americano is a 19th-century Italian cocktail, and, as mixology legends go, the Negroni's precursor. The Americano packs less of a punch; instead of gin, Campari and sweet vermouth are mixed with sparkling water, for a drink beloved by 20th-century spies and 21st-century drinkers seeking low-proof options.

·

20 ml (¾ fl oz) Campari

20 ml (¾ fl oz) sweet vermouth

ice cubes

chilled sparkling water, to top

orange wheel, to garnish

Pour the Campari and sweet vermouth into a highball glass filled with ice. Stir to combine, then top with sparkling water.

Garnish with an orange wheel.

CHAMBORD ROYALE

SERVES 1

Add a splash of Champagne, and you've elevated your drink to a royale. The formula started with kir, but it's a delicious template that works well with any fruit liqueur. In this case, we use Chambord. Produced in France's Loire valley, the liqueur's rich, black raspberry flavour is very sippable. Just add Champagne to finish off this trip to France.

20 ml (¾ fl oz) Chambord

chilled Champagne, to top

1 raspberry on a cocktail stick, to garnish

•

Pour the Chambord into a champagne flute and top with Champagne.

Garnish with the prepared cocktail stick.

BAMBOO

SERVES 1

Fino sherry's a crowd favourite when it comes to the bamboo, but the choice is up to you. Whatever sherry and vermouth you choose to use, equal measures of the fortified wines with a couple of dashes of bitters make this historical cocktail delicious.

·

ice cubes

30 ml (1 fl oz) Fino sherry or other dry sherry

30 ml (1 fl oz) dry vermouth

1 dash of Angostura bitters

1 dash of orange bitters

orange twist, to garnish

In a mixing glass filled with ice, add the sherry, vermouth and bitters. Stir until chillled, then strain into a chilled coupe.

Garnish with an orange twist.

SGROPPINO

SERVES 2

The sgroppino was designed as a palate cleanser, but that doesn't mean you can't enjoy it as a midday treat when the sun's beams are on full blast. Equal parts sweet and tart, this glass of sorbet and Prosecco is the perfect option if you're craving something frosty.

•

Pour the Prosecco into two champagne tulips. Top the glasses with lemon sorbet and garnish with a little lemon zest and a mint sprig.

300 ml (10 fl oz) chilled Prosecco

2 scoops lemon sorbet

lemon zest, to garnish

mint sprig, to garnish

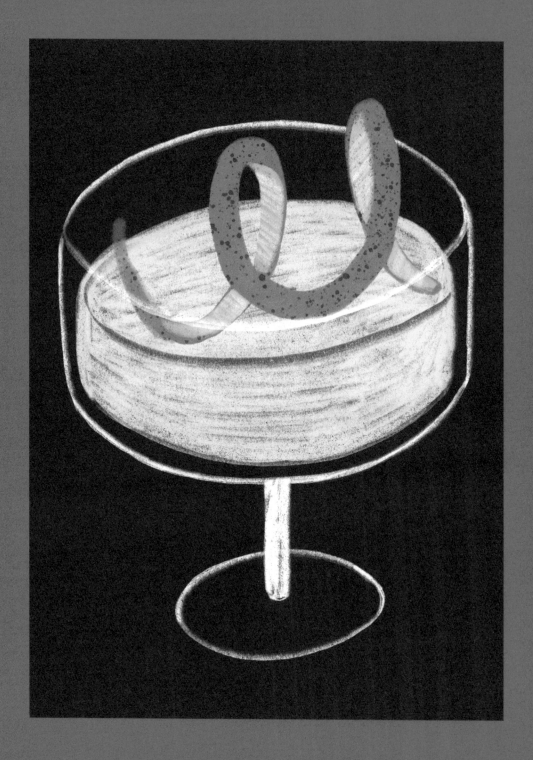

CHRYSANTHEMUM

SERVES 1

ice cubes

40 ml (1¼ fl oz) dry vermouth

1 tablespoon Bénédictine

1 dash of absinthe

chilled sparkling water, to top

orange twist, to garnish

The chrysanthemum is another cocktail classic that relies on fortified wine as its base. The result is a lighter glass that features Bénédictine's herbaceous notes. This liqueur is herbal and tinged with honey, made from a secret recipe that blends 27 herbs and spices. Whatever goes into it, it pairs well with dry vermouth and a hint of absinthe.

•

In a cocktail shaker filled with ice, add the dry vermouth, Bénédictine and absinthe. Shake for 30 seconds, then strain into a chilled cocktail glass. Top with sparkling water.

Serve garnished with an orange twist

SLOE GIN FIZZ

SERVES 1

While sloe gin starts its life at a high ABV, the spirit is infused with sloe berries. In the process, it takes on a ruby hue and loses its high proof, producing a juicier, warmer liqueur. Mix it with sparking water and sugar syrup to make a fizz that highlights sloe gin's tart, fruity notes.

•

30 ml (1 fl oz) sloe gin

20 ml (¾ fl oz) lemon juice

20 ml (¾ fl oz) Sugar syrup
(page 142)

ice cubes

chilled sparkling water, to top

lemon wheel, to garnish

Luxardo maraschino cherry
on a cocktail stick, to garnish

Add the sloe gin, lemon juice and sugar syrup to a cocktail shaker filled with ice, and shake for 30 seconds until well combined. Strain into a highball glass filled with ice and top with sparkling water.

Garnish with a lemon wheel and the maraschino cherry.

ROSE GRANITA

SERVES 8

You don't need a drop of alcohol to make a granita; the Sicilians eat it with brioche in the morning, with a range of flavours, from lemon to coffee. This version eschews tradition, chilling wine in the freezer to create a grown-up snow cone. Add a side of warm brioche to dip into your glass for a classic granita experience.

•

In a large pitcher, combine the sugar, lemon juice and 125 ml (½ cup) of water. Stir for about 1 minute, until the sugar has dissolved. Pour into a shallow 1.25 litre (5 cup) container and add the wine. Stir to combine, then place in the freezer for 1½ hours, or until frozen around the edges.

Stir the granita to combine the frozen edges with the softer mixture in the centre. Freeze for a further 3–4 hours, or until frozen. Break up the mixture with a fork; it should form small ice crystals.

To serve, spoon the granita into serving glasses and enjoy immediately. It will melt as you enjoy it, depending on the room temperature.

The granita will keep in an airtight container in the freezer for up to 4 days.

55 g (¼ cup) caster (superfine) sugar

80 ml (⅓ cup) lemon juice

750 ml (3 cups) chilled bottle of rose

Syrups

SUGAR
MAKES 125 ML (½ CUP)

110 g (4 oz) caster
(superfine) sugar

Combine the sugar and 125 ml (½ cup) of water in a small saucepan. Bring to the boil and stir until the sugar dissolves. Remove from the heat and leave to cool.

The sugar syrup will keep in an airtight container in the fridge for up to 1 week.

VANILLA
MAKES 125 ML (½ CUP)

1 vanilla bean, split open
and seeds scraped

110 g (4 oz) caster
(superfine) sugar

¼ teaspoon vanilla extract
(optional; see page 9)

Combine the vanilla bean and seeds, sugar and 125 ml (½ cup) of water in a saucepan. Bring to the boil and stir until the sugar dissolves. Stir in the vanilla extract, if using, and set aside to cool.

The vanilla syrup will keep in an airtight container in the fridge for up to 1 week.

HONEY
MAKES 125 ML (½ CUP)

90 g (3 oz) honey

1¼ tablespoons chilli flakes (optional)

1 tablespoon apple cider vinegar (optional)

Combine the honey and 60 ml (¼ cup) of water in a small saucepan over low heat. Stir until the honey dissolves, and remove from the heat.

To make hot honey syrup, add the chilli flakes and vinegar. If you like less spice, strain through a fine-mesh sieve into a container after 10 minutes, discarding the solids. If you like your honey hot, leave the chilli flakes in.

The honey syrup will keep in an airtight container in the fridge for up to 1 week.

JUNIPER
MAKES 125 ML (½ CUP)

110 g (4 oz) caster (superfine) sugar

2 tablespoons dried juniper berries

Combine the sugar and 125 ml (½ cup) of water in a small saucepan. Bring to the boil and stir until the sugar dissolves. Remove from the heat and add the juniper berries. Set aside to cool, then strain into a container, discarding the solids.

The juniper syrup will keep in an airtight container in the fridge for 4–5 days.

LAVENDER
MAKES 55 ML (1¾ FL OZ)

55 g (¼ cup) caster (superfine) sugar

2–3 teaspoons dried edible lavender flowers

Combine the sugar, 2 teaspoons of the dried lavender and 60 ml (¼ cup) of water in a small saucepan – add an extra teaspoon of lavender for a stronger flavour. Bring to the boil and stir until the sugar dissolves. Remove from the heat and set aside for 30 minutes to infuse. Strain into a container, discarding the solids.

The lavender syrup will keep in an airtight container in the fridge for 4–5 days.

ELDERFLOWER
MAKES 55 ML (1¾ CUP)

55 g (¼ cup) caster (superfine) sugar

½ cup fresh elderflowers, washed, or 10 g (¼ oz) dried edible elderflowers

zest and juice of ¼ lemon

Combine the sugar and 60 ml (¼ cup) of water in a small saucepan. Bring to the boil and stir until the sugar dissolves. Remove from the heat and add the elderflowers. Leave to cool, then refrigerate for 4 hours, or overnight for a stronger flavour. Strain into a container, discarding the solids.

The elderflower syrup will keep in an airtight container in the fridge for 4–5 days.

ROSE PETAL
MAKES 125 ML (½ CUP)

½ cup dried edible rose petals

115 g (½ cup) caster (superfine) sugar

Combine the rose petals, sugar and 125 ml (½ cup) of water in a small saucepan. Bring to the boil and stir until the sugar dissolves. Remove from the heat and leave to cool, then refrigerate for 4 hours, or overnight for a stronger flavour. Strain into a container, discarding the solids.

The rose petal syrup will keep in an airtight container in the fridge for 4–5 days.

RASPBERRY
MAKES 60 ML (¼ CUP)

55 g (¼ cup) caster (superfine) sugar

5 raspberries

Combine the sugar and 60 ml (¼ cup) of water in a small saucepan. Bring to the boil and stir until the sugar dissolves. Remove from the heat and add the raspberries, using a fork to crush them. Set aside to cool, then strain through a fine-mesh sieve into a container, discarding the solids.

The raspberry syrup will keep in an airtight container in the fridge for up to 5 days.

JALAPENO
MAKES 55 ML (1¾ FL OZ)

55 g (¼ cup) caster (superfine) sugar

1 sliced jalapeno

Combine the sugar, jalapeno and 60 ml (¼ cup) of water in a small saucepan. Bring to the boil and stir until the sugar dissolves. Remove from the heat and set aside for 30 minutes to infuse, then strain through a fine-mesh sieve into a container, discarding the solids.

The jalapeno syrup will keep in an airtight container in the fridge for up to 5 days.

BLACKBERRY
MAKES 125 ML (½ CUP)

110 g (½ cup) sugar

10 blackberries

Combine the sugar and 125 ml (½ cup) of water in a small saucepan. Bring to the boil and stir until the sugar dissolves. Remove from the heat and add the blackberries, using a fork to crush them. Set aside to cool, then strain through a fine-mesh sieve into a container, discarding the solids.

The blackberry syrup will keep in an airtight container in the fridge for up to 5 days.

VELVET FALERNUM

MAKES 125 ML (½ CUP)

1½ teaspoons blanched slivered almonds

10 cloves, crushed

30 ml (1 fl oz) coconut water

zest of 1 lime, plus 2 teaspoons juice

1.5 cm (½ in) piece of ginger, peeled and sliced

55 g (¼ cup) caster (superfine) sugar

¼ teaspoon almond extract

Toast the almonds and cloves in a small dry frying pan over medium heat, until the almonds are golden. Transfer to a container, along with the coconut water, lime zest and ginger. Cover, shake vigorously and let steep at room temperature for 24 hours.

Strain the almond mixture through a sieve lined with muslin (cheesecloth) into a bowl, then squeeze the muslin to get all the oils out of the solids. Discard the solids.

In a jar, add the sugar and 30 ml (1 fl oz) of warm water. Shake until the sugar dissolves. Add the almond mixture, along with the lime juice and almond extract. Shake well to combine.

The falernum syrup will keep in an airtight container in the fridge for up to 5 days.

ORGEAT
MAKES 125 ML
(½ CUP)

60 g (2 oz) raw almonds, soaked in warm water for 30 minutes

90 g (3 oz) caster (superfine) sugar

¼ teaspoon orange blossom water

Drain the almonds and discard the water.

In a food processor, blend the almonds into a paste, adding a little water if needed. Transfer to a bowl and cover with 100 ml (3½ fl oz) of water. Leave to soak for 4 hours.

Over a bowl, strain the almond paste through a sieve lined with muslin (cheesecloth). Squeeze the muslin to extract the almond oils. Return the almond paste to the strained water and leave to soak for another 1–2 hours. Strain and squeeze again. Repeat the process once more if desired, then discard the solids.

In a saucepan over low heat, gently bring the almond water to a simmer. Add the sugar and stir until dissolved. Remove from the heat and set aside to cool, then stir in the orange blossom water.

The orgeat syrup will keep in an container in the fridge for up to 1 week.

ROSEMARY
MAKES 55 ML (1¾ FL OZ)

2 rosemary sprigs, leaves picked and roughly chopped

55 g (¼ cup) caster (superfine) sugar

Combine the rosemary in a small saucepan with the sugar and 60 ml (¼ cup) of water. Bring to the boil and stir until the sugar dissolves. Remove from the heat and leave to infuse for 30 minutes. Strain through a sieve lined with muslin (cheesecloth) into a container, discarding the solids. Allow to cool.

The rosemary syrup will keep in an airtight container in the fridge for 4–5 days.

LIME
MAKES 70 ML (2¼ FL OZ)

55 g (¼ cup) caster (superfine) sugar

zest and juice of 1 lime

Combine the sugar, zest and 60 ml (¼ cup) of water in a small saucepan. Bring to the boil and stir until the sugar dissolves. Remove from the heat and add the juice. Leave to infuse for an hour, then strain through a sieve lined with muslin (cheesecloth) into a container, discarding the solids.

The lime syrup will keep in an airtight container in the fridge for up to 5 days.

Published in 2023 by Smith Street Books
Naarm | Melbourne | Australia
smithstreetbooks.com

ISBN: 978-1-9227-5454-7

All rights reserved. No part of this book may be reproduced
or transmitted by any person or entity, in any form or by any means,
electronic or mechanical, including photocopying, recording, scanning
or by any storage and retrieval system, without the prior written
permission of the publishers and copyright holders.

Smith Street Books respectfully acknowledges the Wurundjeri People
of the Kulin Nation, who are the Traditional Owners of the land on which
we work, and we pay our respects to their Elders past and present.

Copyright text © Smith Street Books
Copyright design © Smith Street Books
Copyright illustrations © Claudia Frittitta

The moral right of the author has been asserted.

Publisher: Paul McNally
Editor and text: Avery Hayes
Illustrations: Claudia Frittitta
Designer: Michelle Mackintosh
Typesetter: Heather Menzies
Proofreader: Ariana Klepac
Indexer: Helena Holmgren

Printed & bound in China by C&C Offset Printing Co., Ltd.

Book 274
10 9 8 7 6 5 4 3 2 1